Lest You Fall

Meditations to Fight Moral Impurity

Rand Hummel

journeyforth®

Greenville, South Carolina

Library of Congress Cataloging-in-Publication Data

Hummel, Rand, 1956-
  Lest you fall / Rand Hummel.
      p. cm.
  Summary: "This is a study on how meditation can help a person have victory
over impurity"—Provided by publisher.
  Includes index.
  ISBN 1-59166-465-9 (perfect bound pbk. : alk. paper)
  1. Meditation—Christianity. 2. Holiness—Christianity. 3. Sex—Religious
aspects—Christianity. I. Title.

  BV4813.H65 2005
  248.3'4—dc22

                                                            2005006905

Cover Photo Credits: Comstock Images (front, back)

The fact that materials produced by other publishers may be referred to in
this volume does not constitute an endorsement of the content or theological
position of materials produced by such publishers.

All Scripture is quoted from the Authorized King James Version.

Lest You Fall: Meditations to Fight Moral Impurity

Design by Jeff Gray
Composition by Melissa Matos

© 2005 by BJU Press
Greenville, South Carolina 29614
JourneyForth Books is a division of BJU Press

ISBN 978-1-59166-465-9

15 14 13 12 11 10 9 8 7

Table of Contents

Introduction

Dear Reader,

As the title of the book clearly states, we must all take heed, watch out, and be careful . . . lest we fall! Failure in areas of immorality has almost become epidemic. With the constant bombardment of sexual temptations attacking God's people from every avenue of life, we must be aggressive in our fight for personal purity.

The simple meditations found in this book are designed to get us to meditate on the very words of God in such a way that the deceitfulness and wickedness of sin are clearly exposed and that hope for victory over impurity is realized. How can men and women today cleanse their way? By taking heed, guarding their hearts and minds with the very words of God.

Please do not get in a hurry. Take your time even if it means taking three years to get through this book. Think. Meditate. Spend time with each word and word meaning until the truth of what God is saying becomes a part of your life.

Remember, there is no excuse to sin. "There hath no temptation taken you but such as is common to man: but God is faithful, who will not suffer you to be tempted above that ye are able; but will with the temptation also make a way to escape, that ye may be able to bear it" (1 Cor. 10:13). Meditating on the truths of God's Word dealt with in this book can be your way of escape.

Don't fall,

Take heed, watch out, be careful . . .

Lest you fall

Rand Hummel

Meditation

Let's think about it.

Meditation is essential for anyone who desires to stay pure. The word translated "meditation" throughout Scripture is also translated "imagine" (Ps. 2:1; 38:12), "studieth" (Prov. 15:28; 24:2), "utter, mutter, talk, or speak" (Job 27:4; Ps. 37:30; 71:24; Prov. 8:7), and "mourn" (Isa. 16:7; 38:14; 59:11). It is usually defined as "murmuring," or speaking to oneself. How often do we as believers devote a full morning to studying, imagining, talking through, or speaking to ourselves (meditating) about one specific characteristic of God taught in His Word?

1

Meditation is a form of creative thinking. Through word studies, comparisons with other passages, and a good study Bible we can understand what God is saying and how to apply it in a life-changing way. For instance, if we set aside an entire hour to "think about" or meditate on how much God loves righteousness and hates evil, our thinking will be affected in such a way that we will personally begin loving good and hating evil more.

Meditation is essential for a full understanding of God's Word. Most of us have developed lazy habits in reading, grammar, syntax, and word study. We often glance over a word we think we know rather than gaze into its true intent and purpose. When Paul uses the phrase "for this cause" (Rom. 1:26; Eph. 5:31; 2 Thess. 2:11, and so forth) it is so easy to keep reading rather than to stop and think, "What cause?" "What is this driving force in Paul's life?" "What was his essential reason for living?" "What is my ultimate reason, purpose, or cause for living?" "Have I attached myself to a cause bigger than myself, my wants, my time, and my life?" Now, Paul's simple phrase "for this cause" takes on a new relevance, and my heart is convicted because I have been living for my own "causes" and not God's!

Meditation is essential for all who seek victory over sexual temptations. Failure in sexual temptations may come from a lack of knowledge, a misunderstanding of Bible principles, or a misapplication of scriptural truth. Many of the passages that deal with the sins of immorality we have read but not thought about in a way that impacts our hearts. How should Hebrews 13:4–5 influence us as we sit face to face with a sensual television show or a pornographic website? The purpose of this book is to encourage those who desire to stay pure to meditate on the very words God wants us to hear that deal with fleshly temptations. What God has already given us in His written Word are the very words He would speak to us if we were in a one-on-one counseling situation. As you will see, many passages dealing with personal purity will be dealt with in a meditative way. At the end of this book, you can take what you have learned and begin meditating on other passages of Scripture in the same way.

Meditation is a form of creative thinking.

We can live pure, holy lives, free from bondage or enslavement to sexual sins as we begin thinking like God thinks. That takes time. That takes energy. That takes meditation! Now, let's think about it.

"Meditate upon these things; give thyself wholly to them; that thy profiting may appear to all" *(1 Tim. 4:15)*.

Meditation should delight us!

"I will meditate in thy precepts, and have respect unto thy ways. I will delight myself in thy statutes: I will not forget thy word" *(Ps. 119:15–16)*.

"Blessed is the man that walketh not in the counsel of the ungodly, nor standeth in the way of sinners, nor sitteth in the seat of the scornful. But his delight is in the law of the Lord; and in his law doth he meditate day and night" *(Ps. 1:1–2)*.

"My meditation of him shall be sweet: I will be glad in the Lord" *(Ps. 104:34)*.

Meditation should consume us!

"Let the words of my mouth, and the meditation of my heart, be acceptable in thy sight, O Lord, my strength, and my redeemer" *(Ps. 19:14)*.

"O how love I thy law! It is my meditation all the day" *(Ps. 119:97).*

"Mine eyes prevent the night watches, that I might meditate in thy word" *(Ps. 119:148).*

Meditation should control us!

"This book of the law shall not depart out of thy mouth; but thou shalt meditate therein day and night, that thou mayest observe to do according to all that is written therein: for then thou shalt make thy way prosperous, and then thou shalt have good success" *(Josh. 1:8).*

The Mechanics of Meditation

"How do you do this?"

In some times of life, there is danger in being a "do-it-yourselfer." I know enough about working on cars to get a job started but often not enough to finish it. Some "do-it-yourself" plumbers, with the goal of simply replacing a faucet, can turn a bathroom into a water park complete with fountains and pools. There are other times when it is essential to be a "do-it-yourselfer." Meditation is one of those times. It is something that we must learn to do ourselves. We can read books, listen to messages, and allow others to meditate for us or we can study, labor, and master the art of meditation for ourselves. This is definitely a do-it-yourself discipline of the Christian life.

Anyone can meditate. Everyone should meditate. Most don't even try. If you were not interested in staying pure and learning to meditate on what God has to say about purity, you probably would not even be reading this book. What you need is a meditation toolbox that is filled with the proper meditation tools. I would encourage you to get one tool at a time and practice using it until you have mastered it. Don't fall into the trap of filling your toolbox with specialty tools that you never use.

Tool 1: Your Bible

Read . . . read . . . READ! Read the passage you are studying over and over again. I sometimes type the book or passage out to myself in letter form without any verse or chapter markings. I start with the letter addressed to myself.

> *Dear Rand,*
>
> *Type the passage and then end the letter with—*
>
> *Your friend,*
> *Paul, Peter, John, or whoever*

Tool 2: A study Bible

Study Bibles are a tremendous help in understanding the intent and purpose of any given passage. Sometimes a simple clarification of the audience, customs, geographical considerations, or unusual word usages can help you to understand what God was saying to those people at that time. Bible scholars have given their lives to help those who may not have the time or the training to fully understand why God wrote what He wrote in His Word.

Tool 3: Word-study helps

There are many words in our English Bible whose meanings have changed over the years and have almost become obsolete in conversation today. Words such as *concupiscence, superfluity, wantonness, lasciviousness, lucre, guile,* and *quickened* are not found in most of the letters or e-mails we read on a daily basis. Word-study helps such as *Strong's Concordance, Vines Expository Dictionary, Robertson's New Testament Word Pictures, Vincent's New Testament Word Studies, Theological Wordbook of the Old Testament,* and Greek and Hebrew lexicons open up the meanings to words we commonly glance over as we read. Words are powerful. Because we often do not know the true meanings of certain words, we miss their intent and cannot personally apply the passage as we should.

Tool 4: Bible dictionaries and encyclopedias

Most of us have not grown up in the Holy Land, lived in Egypt, or sailed the Mediterranean. I personally have never fished with a net, hunted with a bow, or plowed with an ox. A good Bible dictionary or encyclopedia can help you feel the heat of the desert and understand the difficulty of sailing through a stormy sea. I would suggest *ISBE (International Standard Bible Encyclopedia), Zondervan Pictorial Bible Dictionary, Nelson's New Illustrated Bible Dictionary,* or *Unger's Bible Dictionary* to start with.

Tool 5: Commitment of time

All the tools available are to no avail without a commitment of time and a commitment to concentration. Meditation takes time. We seem to have the time to do what we want but not the time to do what we should. Consistency in spending extended periods of time in

God's Word is a key to proper meditation. Anytime is a good time, but if you give God, say, one-half hour every morning before you get pulled into your fast and furious daily routine, you will actually wake up in the morning looking forward to spending that time with God. (By the way, if you think you are too busy, consider that this kind of meditation in God's Word will simply replace the wasted time it takes to sin.)

Tool 6: A set place

Finding the right place to ensure complete concentration is also a must. Unless you have a set place to meditate, distractions can easily cause your mind to drift. Find a place where you are isolated, or at least insulated, from the distractions of TV, newspapers, radio, children, friends, and weariness. Find a place where it is just you and God and it is almost as though the whole world disappears for those few minutes each morning.

Tool 7: Prayer

Talk to God. Ask God to open your eyes and your heart to what He is saying. Ask God for wisdom; He promises to give it to you. Ask God for understanding; He wants you to understand. Ask God for insight into His heart. Ask God to help you think as He thinks, to look at sin as He looks at sin, to love purity as He loves purity. Your goal is to stay pure by having the mind of Christ. When your meditation becomes your mindset, you will be amazed at your understanding of Scripture and your progress in consistent victory over selfish, sinful thinking. You'll also be pleasing God and not self.

Before we step into the heart of this book, let's walk through one short passage using the tools mentioned above. What is God saying to us in Proverbs 5:22? What words do we need to study and understand so that we do not miss their meaning and intent? What word pictures do these words bring to mind that will help us not only fully understand what they are saying but also apply in such a way that they evoke a stronger love for God and purity and an intense hatred for sin?

This is what God says.

Proverbs 5:22

His own iniquities shall take the wicked himself,
and he shall be holden with the cords of his sins.

Now think about it.

Who is *his*, *himself*, *he*, and *his* referring to? (This is
where you look at the sentence grammatically to find
out who these personal pronouns are referring to. This
one is easy. They are all pointing to a wicked person.) A
wicked, sinful, selfish person. A person just like you and
me! What are iniquities and sins? (Studying your Strong's
concordance or a Bible dictionary will reveal not only that
iniquity is sin but also that in the Old Testament it has the
concept of worthless or nothing—a moral worthlessness.
It is foolish, vain, and worthless and does absolutely nothing good for your life and relationship with God. Those
involved in iniquity are simply wasting their lives away.
Sin is defiant rebellion against God. It is choosing your
way above God's way. It is making a god of yourself, worshiping yourself, putting yourself in an esteemed position
above the true God.)

What are the words *take*, *holden*, and *cords* referring to? The word *take* according to Strong's means "to catch in a net, trap, or pit; to capture." The word *holden* means "to keep or to restrain." Cords are best described as something that is intertwined as a noose or ropes that confine or shackle. Put these three words together and you think of either a hunter trying to trap game, a medieval enemy seeking to capture and imprison slaves in a damp, dark dungeon, or a life of imprisonment as a wicked criminal behind bars. All three examples involve captivity or servitude. These word pictures help to understand and apply this simple verse.

How can this affect me?

Who wants to be entrapped and destroyed like a wild animal? Who would volunteer to be the slave of a selfish, lying, uncaring master? Who wants to be treated like an imprisoned criminal? Who wants to spend the rest of his life in prison, separated from his wife and kids, forgotten by his friends and coworkers, surrounded by ungodly men who have experimented and perfected every sexual perversion imaginable with their depraved minds? The answer? The person who refuses to stop pleasing himself with his filthy imaginations and to start pleasing God with purity of mind and body. Do you really want to be a slave to sin for the rest of your life?

The more you meditate, the better you will become at meditation. It really does not take too long to become somewhat of a pro. After a while, you will find yourself simply reading a passage as your mind begins to race with synonyms, word pictures, explanations, applications, and illustrations. Your meditation toolbox will gradually fill with your favorite tools, whether they live on your bookshelf or hide on the hard drive of your computer. Your understanding, teaching, preaching, counseling, and everyday life fellowshiping will be enriched by your grasp of God's Word.

The more you meditate, the better you will become at it.

The rest of this book will simply illustrate and give examples of the application of the mechanics of meditation. May we all agree with what David shared in Psalm 119:97, "O how love I thy law! it is my meditation all the day."

Meditation 1

Do you really want to be a slave to sin?
This is what God says.

Proverbs 7:22–23

He goeth after her straightway, as an ox goeth to the
slaughter, or as a fool to the correction of the stocks;
till a dart strike through his liver; as a bird hasteth
to the snare, and knoweth not that it is for his life.

Now think about it.

Straightway, immediately, all at once, without fighting the temptation at all, he chased after that which he

thought would satisfy his sexual desires with as much sense as an ox that hurries toward the butcher who has some tasty grain in his one hand to lure it and a knife in the other ready to take its life, or as a nonthinking deer that steps into a bear trap, holding it captive until the hunter shoots his bow, sending an arrow of death straight through its liver, or as a bird that flies straight into a snare, not knowing that the hunter put the snare in that very place to catch and kill it.

How can this affect me?

Those caught up in sexual addiction are quite impulsive. They act first and think later. When they are faced with any sexual temptation, from filthy pornography to a promiscuous person, they "straightway" run to the sin without any thought of the consequences. All they desire is the instant satisfaction the flesh so deceitfully cries for. They are blinded to the fact that you cannot sin and win. The immoral butcher is ready to slit their throat, and the seducing hunter has his arrow ready to fly through the heart of the unsuspecting sexual addict. Satan will attempt to kill and destroy every man or woman he can get his wicked hands on. He uses immorality as the bait and, sadly to say, often bags his limit. Satan would love to add you to his list of trophies. He wants you dead.

This is what God says.

2 Peter 2:10, 14, 18–19

But chiefly them that walk after the flesh in the lust of uncleanness, and despise government. Presumptuous are they, selfwilled, they are not afraid to speak evil of dignities. . . . Having eyes full of adultery, and that cannot cease from sin; beguiling unstable souls: an heart they have exercised with covetous practices; cursed children. . . . For when they speak great swelling words of vanity, they allure through the lusts of the flesh, through much wantonness, those that were clean escaped from them who live in error. While they promise them liberty, they themselves are the servants of corruption: for of whom a man is overcome, of the same is he brought in bondage.

Now think about it.

God will be especially hard on those who walk after the flesh in the lust of uncleanness, follow their own evil, corrupt, lustful desires, and despise all authority or anyone else who tries to tell them that they are in sin. They are so presumptuous, proud, bold, and arrogant that they are not afraid to speak evil of, slander, or scoff at anyone.

These are the ones who are trying so hard to escape . . .

They feast their eyes on adultery through pornographic magazines, movies, and Internet sites, and are so addicted to committing adultery and fornication in their minds they cannot quit or cease from sin; they beguile, seduce, entice, and make a game of getting unstable, weak, and unsuspecting people to join them in their filthy immorality; they have exercised their hearts through hours of practicing their sin and have become experts in greed and covetousness, desiring people and pleasures God never intended them to have; and even though they may not know it, they have made choices that could doom and curse them for eternity . . . For when they speak great swelling words of vanity and brag about themselves with empty, foolish boasting, they

18

try to allure or coax others to be involved in their sin by appealing to their fleshly desires. These are the ones who are trying so hard to escape from following such empty, lewd, and fleshly lifestyles. While those who are addicted to habitual, sexual sin promise them freedom and liberty, trying to make them believe that they are free to live out any sexual desire they have, they themselves are slaves to their sexual idols and servants of their depravity and corruption: for of whom a man is overcome, of the same is he brought into bondage, for you are a slave to whatever controls you.

How can this affect me?

Not only do those consumed with sexual sin have filthy minds but they are also out of their minds. They don't think clearly! They think they are free to do whatever they want but cannot see that they are actually slaves. They have lied to themselves, justifying their own sin so many times that they think they are doing others a favor by getting them to join them in their sin. They choose not to think about the first few words of 2 Peter 2:10. God is going to be especially hard in the way He deals with them.

They may believe they are free and having fun, but their judgment day is quickly approaching. Can you imagine what it will be like for those who spend their entire lives satisfying fleshly desires to someday explain their choices to God?

This is what God says.

Proverbs 26:11

As a dog returneth to his vomit, so a fool returneth to his folly.

Now think about it.

As a dog goes back to eat its own vomit, so a fool repeats his foolish sin over and over again.

How can this affect me?

This has got to be one of the grossest pictures of habitual sin I can think of. The cycle never stops. A dog eats, gets sick, throws up in the grass, eats it again, gets sick again, throws it up again, eats it again, and so forth. A dog never seems to learn. Even if it hates eating its own vomit, it still does it over and over again. Those on the edge of sexual addiction do the same thing. Even though they sometimes hate what they're doing, they do it anyway. These are the individuals who go to God over and over asking for forgiveness for the ten-thousandth time. The constant repetition of the same sin reveals not only a man's foolishness and weakness but also his real heart's desire. He obviously loves himself and his sin much more than he loves his God. That is why he goes back to his nauseating sin over and over and over. If you, like the dog we read about today, repeatedly go back to the same habitual sin, you are headed for a big fall. Repeating the same sick sin over and over should make you sick. It makes God sick.

Meditation 2

What are "the lusts of the heart"?

Desire is not bad. When we commit our lives to God, He gives us the "desires" of our heart. God-given desire is often what motivates us to seek and fulfill God's will. If God had not created us with a desire to eat and drink, we would starve or die of thirst. If God had not given us the desire for sex, procreation would come to a halt. When such appetites are corrupted by sin, they become imbalanced and controlling. Lust can be defined as "desiring something God forbids us to have." Lust is a desire that focuses on satisfying self and no one else, not even God. Sinful lust cannot be blamed on parents, environment, hormone imbalance, demons, or society. James 1:14 clearly tells us where our lust comes from, "But every man is tempted, when he is drawn away of his own lust!" Intense passion for the forbidden may give you what you want, but it will take away and destroy everything you already have.

This is what God says.

LUST IS DECEITFUL.

Ephesians 4:22

That ye put off concerning the former conversation the old man, which is corrupt according to the deceitful lusts.

Now think about it.

Stop living a sinful, selfish lifestyle. Do not let your old corrupt nature (which is rotten through and through) continue to ruin your life by its deceitful lusts and desires.

This is what God says.

LUST IS FOOLISH AND HURTFUL.

1 Timothy 6:9

But they that will be rich fall into temptation and a snare, and into many foolish and hurtful lusts, which drown men in destruction and perdition.

Now think about it.

Those who have a driving desire to be rich easily fall into all kinds of temptations and are literally trapped by their empty, harmful, and hurtful lusts, which plunge men into the depths of ruin and destruction.

This is what God says.

LUST IS CONTROLLING.

Romans 6:12

Let not sin therefore reign in your mortal body, that ye should obey it in the lusts thereof.

Now think about it.

Refuse to permit sin to be your king and reign over your flesh like a tyrant who gives you no choice but to obey and give in to its unquenchable lusts and desires.

This is what God says.

LUST IS AT WAR WITH YOUR SOUL.

1 Peter 2:11

Dearly beloved, I beseech you as strangers and pilgrims, abstain from fleshly lusts, which war against the soul.

Now think about it.

My dearly loved brothers and sisters in Christ, as we are essentially aliens and foreigners in this world and should never feel at home with the sin this world has to offer, I plead with you to stay as far away from evil desires and fleshly lusts as you possibly can. These intense lusts constantly fight against you and have waged war against your very soul. Please, please stay away.

This is what God says.

LUST IS FILTHY.

2 Peter 2:9–10

The Lord knoweth how to deliver the godly out of temptations, and to reserve the unjust unto the day of judgment to be punished: but chiefly them that walk after the flesh in the lust of uncleanness, and despise government. Presumptuous are they, selfwilled, they are not afraid to speak evil of dignities.

Now think about it.

The Lord knows how to rescue and deliver the godly out of temptation and how to keep the ungodly under punishment until their day of judgment, but He will be especially hard on those who continue to indulge in filthy lusts and fleshly desires while despising and looking down on all authority. They are proud, arrogant, self-willed individuals who not only despise God's authority but are daring enough to scoff at God's powerful angels.

This is what God says.

LUST IS AT WAR INSIDE OF YOU.

James 4:1

From whence come wars and fightings among you? come they not hence, even of your lusts that war in your members?

Now think about it.

What is actually causing all the quarreling and fighting among you? Isn't it the whole army of evil desires and fleshly lusts that are at war inside of you?

This is what God says.

LUST WILL KILL YOU.

James 1:14–16

But every man is tempted, when he is drawn away of his own lust, and enticed. Then when lust hath conceived, it bringeth forth sin: and sin, when it is finished, bringeth forth death. Do not err, my beloved brethren.

Now think about it.

Mark it down, every man, even you, will be tempted. (You cannot keep from being tempted, but you can determine ahead of time what you are going to do when the temptation comes. You cannot just resist; you must run.) When your own lust and evil desires grab hold of your attention, you are lured, enticed, and drawn to committing the sin. Then, once your controlling lust takes root in your heart, it matures into full-grown sin as you rebel against God and His Word; and remember, when that sin is finished, it brings death. It will kill you. Do not be deceived, thinking that you can get away with your sin, my dearly loved brothers and sisters in Christ.

How can this affect me?

Lust is deceitful.

Lust is foolish and hurtful.

Lust is controlling.

Lust is at warfare with your soul.

Lust is filthy.

Lust is at war inside of you.

Lust will kill you.

Meditation 3

Love gives. Lust takes.
This is what God says.

Ephesians 5:1–4

Be ye therefore followers of God, as dear children: and walk in love, as Christ also hath loved us, and hath given himself for us an offering and a sacrifice to God for a sweet-smelling savor. But fornication, and all uncleanness, or covetousness, let it not be once named among you, as becometh saints; neither filthiness, nor foolish talking, nor jesting, which are not convenient: but rather giving of thanks.

Now think about it.

Just as a small, dearly loved child imitates his father, you too are dearly loved of God; therefore, be an imitator of God; and just like Jesus Christ loved us, giving of Himself and not taking for Himself, live a life that is filled with unselfish love for others and not selfish love for yourself. Jesus Christ loved us so much that He gave His life by dying for us, as an offering or payment for our sin, and God was well pleased with His fragrant, sweet-smelling sacrifice. Just as Christ left us the example, we are to walk in love. But all sexual immorality, ranging from filling your mind with pornographic trash to being unfaithful to your marriage commitment of purity (fornication), and all impurity that comes from walking through the sewer of sexual filth and perversion (uncleanness), or greedily desiring sexual satisfaction in a way that God never intended (covetousness), let it not be once named among you, as becometh saints. Such sinful behavior should have no part in the lives of God's holy people; neither should there ever be filthy, obscene, sexually suggestive conversations, nor foolish, empty, silly talk, nor coarse jesting and dirty jokes. These are totally out of place for any

Christian; but rather there should be giving of thanks to a God who wants what is best for us. He wants us to walk in love and not in lust.

How can this affect me?

Walk in love, not in lust.

Love builds relationships that last.	Lust destroys relationships with others and with God.
Love is holy, comforting, and totally focused on Christ and others.	Lust is crude, dirty, and totally focused on the lustful individual.
Love is concerned for others.	Lust is self-focused.
If you walk in love, you will live with the freedom and the confidence of a clean mind.	If you walk in lust, you will be bound by the shackles of guilt and the never-ending lustful desire for more and more.
Love satisfies.	Lust is never satisfied.

Walk in love, not in lust.

Meditation 4

There are no secret sins!

This is what God says.

Luke 8:17

For nothing is secret, that shall not be made manifest; neither any thing hid, that shall not be known and come abroad.

Now think about it.

Nothing, *nothing* is secret, that will not be revealed or made known to others; neither is anything concealed or hidden, that will not be known, come to light, and brought out into the open for all to see.

How can this affect me?

Those who have nothing to hide, hide nothing. What are you hiding? What is in your secret life that would destroy your testimony and devastate your relationships with others if they found out? What secrets are hidden in your private life? What do you and God know about you that no one else on earth knows? God says that whatever is secret today will someday be known by all . . . yes, your friends, your family, and everyone else who really cares about you. Then what will they think?

This is what God says.

Luke 12:2–3

For there is nothing covered, that shall not be revealed; neither hid, that shall not be known. Therefore whatsoever ye have spoken in darkness shall be heard in the light; and that which ye have spoken in the ear in closets shall be proclaimed upon the housetops.

Now think about it.

For there is nothing covered, nothing concealed, that will not be revealed; neither hid, that shall not be known. Your secret sins may not be as secret as you think they are. Whatever you have done or are doing will be found out by others. Therefore whatever conversations you have had when you thought no one would ever know will come out; and what you have secretly whispered to strangers on the street, or coworkers at the office, or immoral men and women over the phone or in chat rooms will be proclaimed or shouted from the housetops.

How can this affect me?

There are no secret sins. If you think you have been able to cover your tracks, it is just a matter of time before you will be found out. Don't fool yourself into thinking that it is okay to talk about sensuality as long as you do not physically take part in it. Ephesians 5:12 says, "For it is a shame even to speak of those things which are done of them in secret." Satan wants to entrap you and to expose you in order to ruin your testimony and bring shame on the name of our holy God. Remember, what you whisper in private will be shouted in public. There are no secrets.

This is what God says.

Isaiah 29:13, 15

Wherefore the Lord said, Forasmuch as this people draw near me with their mouth, and with their lips do honour me, but have removed their heart far from me, and their fear toward me is taught by the precept of men. . . . Woe unto them that seek deep to hide their counsel from the Lord, and their works are in the dark, and they say, Who seeth us? and who knoweth us?

Now think about it.

Listen closely to what the Lord says, These people draw near Me with their mouth, they *say* they are Mine, and with their lips they honor Me, pretending that everything in their lives and relationship with Me is just fine, but because of their habitual sin and selfishness, they are about as far from Me as a man can get. They have removed their heart far from me by proudly choosing to love what I hate.

Their pride forces Me to resist them and keep My blessing and protection from them. Their fear and worship of Me is nothing more than a bunch of traditional formalities, rules, and regulations taught by phony spiritual leaders. If you think life is hard now, woe to all of you who try to hide your premeditated plans to be involved in your sexual escapades from the Lord. Certain destruction will come on all who think they can keep God in the dark so that He does not know what is going on. Obviously, if you think or believe "The Lord can't see us!" or "God does not know what I am doing right now!" you don't know God very well.

How can this affect me?

Even if you can keep your filthy thought life or sexual sins secret from your family and friends, you cannot hide them from God. He knows! He sees everything you do! If you are truly a child of God, the only reason you have not experienced His correction is His longsuffering and compassion. If your heart is consumed and controlled with fleshly desires, and your only fear is getting caught and embarrassed, your relationship with God is basically nonexistent. You may have faked a personal relationship with God for so long that you believe your own lie. Does this describe you? If it does, you are headed for a big fall.

This is what God says.

Ezekiel 8:9–12

And he said unto me, Go in, and behold the wicked abominations that they do here. So I went in and saw; and behold every form of creeping things, and abominable beasts, and all the idols of the house of Israel, pourtrayed upon the wall round about. And there stood before them seventy men of the ancients of the house of Israel, and in the midst of them stood Jaazaniah the son of Shaphan, with every man his censer in his hand; and a thick cloud of incense went up. Then said he unto me, Son of man, hast thou seen what the ancients of the house of Israel do in the dark, every man in the chamber of his imagery? for they say, The Lord seeth us not; the Lord hath forsaken the earth.

Now think about it.

In a vision, God told me to go into a temple room to see the unspeakable wickedness that those professing to know God were doing. So I went in, looked around, and could not believe what I saw; on the walls there were graffiti, pictures, and words depicting the perverse forms of idolatrous worship that were detestable in the eyes of God. And there stood before these pictures, seventy ancient men (older men, men who knew better, men who knowingly turned their back on God to be involved in fleshly, self-satisfying worship) from the house of Israel (who were supposed to know and love God), and right in the middle of them stood Jaazaniah, the son of Shaphan, who also worshiped the detestable pictures portrayed on the walls. (Shaphan read the Word of God to King Josiah during a great revival; Jaazaniah heard his father read God's Word. He knew the Word of God just like many of us but chose to rebel against it and live for himself.) Then God said, Ezekiel, have you seen what the spiritual leaders of Israel are doing in the dark when they think no one can see, each man in the rooms of his imagination? These ungodly men foolishly say, The Lord can't see us; the Lord has turned His back on everyone on earth.

How can this affect me?

The ease and availability of pornography on the Internet has certainly had its effects on God's people today. It used to be filthy, dirty old men who would sneak around adult bookstores to find the printed sewage. Now, all anyone has to do is go home, make sure no one is around, and dive into the despicable depths of Internet pornography. Every wicked perversion is available online. There are images hidden in the dark side of the Internet that would be illegal to sell in adult bookstores today! Obviously, you know something about God and His Word or you would not be reading this book. Even though you know what God loves and what He hates, are you still choosing to be involved in that which is an abomination in His eyes? Have you deceived yourself into thinking that pornography is no big deal to God and that He is not concerned with what is going on in your life? God does see and is very concerned. He knows what kind of wickedness will consume your heart and tear it away from Him. There are no secret sins with God. Please acknowledge God's presence (and grief); confess, and repent of your sin. God never overlooks sin; neither does He overlook a contrite heart.

Meditation 5

Is there a point of no return? Are you there?
This is what God says.
Romans 1:21–22

Because that, when they knew God, they glorified him not as God, neither were thankful; but became vain in their imaginations, and their foolish heart was darkened. Professing themselves to be wise, they became fools.

Now think about it.

Yes, these immoral men knew God, but they refused to worship Him as God by giving Him any honor or thanks;

they became vain in their imaginations and futile in their thinking by conjuring up foolish ideas of what God was like and what He would allow them to do, and as their foolish hearts were darkened, their minds became more and more filthy and confused. Professing themselves to be wise, they really thought they knew what they were doing and actually believed themselves to be wiser than God, but they became utter fools instead, not knowing where their selfishness and sensuality would lead them.

How can this affect me?

The minute we get our eyes off God and on our selfish desires, we are precariously standing on the top edge of a very steep cliff of covetousness. God knows what will truly satisfy and bring fulfillment to our lives. When we do not recognize God's provision and thank Him for what He already has given us, we start sliding down that slippery slope of discontentment. Those who are consistently involved in sexual sin of any kind are, in essence, turning their backs on God and stepping onto a slope that will send them sliding away from God faster and farther than they ever intended to go.

This is what God says.

Romans 1:24–28

Wherefore God also gave them up to uncleanness through the lusts of their own hearts, to dishonour their own bodies between themselves: who changed the truth of God into a lie, and worshipped and served the creature more than the Creator, who is blessed for ever. Amen. For this cause God gave them up unto vile affections: for even their women did change the natural use into that which is against nature: and likewise also the men, leaving the natural use of the woman, burned in their lust one toward another; men with men working that which is unseemly, and receiving in themselves that recompence of their error which was meet. And even as they did not like to retain God in their knowledge, God gave them over to a reprobate mind, to do those things which are not convenient.

Now think about it.

Wherefore God also gave up on those who turned their backs on Him so that they could feed their sexual

42

addiction with uncleanness. He let them do whatever shameful, wicked thing their hearts desired, to dishonor and degrade their own bodies between themselves by being involved in perverse, wicked sexual sin: who changed the truth of God into a lie, or in other words, deliberately chose to believe lies even though they knew the truth about God and worshipped and served the creature more than the Creator, who is blessed for ever. Amen. Because of their self-worship (which is essentially the root cause of all sexual sin), God gave them over to shameful lusts, vile passions and selfish loves: for even their women twisted God's natural plan

Who changed the truth of God into a lie . . .

and in rebellion against man and God started sleeping with each other, which is against nature, and so did the men. Instead of having normal and natural sexual relations with women, they burned in their lust toward other men and fell farther down that slippery slope of sin. They looked for sexual fulfillment in homosexuality and acted out their fantasies in indecent, shameful, and perverted behavior. They received in themselves that recompence of their error which was meet; in other words, they suffered the penalty they deserved. Because they insisted on

43

turning their backs on the truth they knew was from God and lived in their habitual sexual sin, God gave them what they wanted and also gave up on them to let them live and die in their sin. And even as they did not like to retain God in their knowledge, even though they did not want to think about God and purity, even though they insisted on pushing God out of their minds with filthy thinking and sexual fantasies, God gave them over to a reprobate, depraved, debased, filthy mind, to do those things which should never, ever be done by mankind. What things? Well, homosexuality is just the tip of the iceberg. Don't be surprised if your burning lust motivates you even to contemplate criminal acts against women and children such as rape and sexual abuse. This is the dark and despicable end of the slope of sin that leads us away from God.

How can this affect me?

The slippery slope into habitual sexual sin is fast . . . so fast you can hardly catch your breath. As many look back up the slope from where they came, they cannot believe where their sin has led them, but they also decide it is too far and too hard to climb back up. So they accept their new lifestyle . . . life without God! Even though those who truly know God would never plan this ahead of time, their sin completely takes over their lives. It is not that they say no to God; they simply choose to forget that there is a God. On the other hand, there are some who have looked back up the slope and have wanted to climb out of the hole they have thrown themselves into. They have put off their old ungodly habits and have begun renewing their minds with God's Word. Because of this, they have been able to put on new godly habits. They have made it back up the slippery slope. But it is a long, hard climb, and the scars they received on the trip down never go away. Take heed, watch out, be careful to stay away from the edge of that slippery slope of sin . . . lest you fall.

This is what God says.

Romans 1:32

Who knowing the judgment of God, that they which commit such things are worthy of death, not only do the same, but have pleasure in them that do them.

Now think about it.

Even though they are fully aware of God's judgment, which is the death penalty against those who habitually practice their sexual fantasies and sins, they not only choose to do those sinful things anyway but also approve and have pleasure in them that do them.

How can this affect me?

If you are involved in immorality on any level, from the mind games that are played with pornography and the media to the violation of the vows and commitments you have made or will make to your spouse someday, you can never plead ignorance. You know better. You are not an exception. You know that God hates all sexual sin! If you continue down the slope toward sexual addiction, the day will come when you will not only be involved in unimaginable acts of perversion but you will also applaud others living in rebellion against God. Do not take pleasure in other men's sins. It will destroy you.

Meditation 6

What hope do those living in life-dominating sin have for eternal life?

How can these passages affect me?

A Christian can slip and commit sin ... any sin. But how often does someone have to sin before it becomes a habitual, life-dominating sin? How long does someone have to live in sin before one can determine that he cannot possibly have the Spirit of God dwelling inside of him? Personally, I am not sure. But knowing what God says in Ephesians 5:5–6, Galatians 5:19–21, and 1 Corinthians 6:9–11, it is very foolish to choose to be involved in habitual sexual sin knowing that the question of where you will spend eternity is always hanging over your head! Only God knows your heart for sure. It is desperately wicked and can fool even you at times. If you are addicted to sexual sin, you had better seriously meditate on the following passages. For you, it could be a matter of spiritual life or death.

This is what God says.

Ephesians 5:5–6

For this ye know, that no whoremonger, nor unclean person, nor covetous man, who is an idolater, hath any inheritance in the kingdom of Christ and of God. Let no man deceive you with vain words: for because of these things cometh the wrath of God upon the children of disobedience.

Now think about it.

Here is one thing that you can be absolutely sure about—no habitually immoral (whoremonger), impure (unclean), or greedy (covetous) person will inherit the kingdom of Christ and of God. For those greedily seeking for more and more sensual pleasures are actually idolaters, worshiping sex and bowing before the altar of this sensual god. Don't let anyone talk you out of this with foolish logic and empty words: for this very reason alone, God's wrath comes on those who disobey and refuse to submit to God's standards of morality.

This is what God says.

Galatians 5:19–21

Now the works of the flesh are manifest, which are these; Adultery, fornication, uncleanness, lasciviousness, idolatry, witchcraft, hatred, variance, emulations, wrath, strife, seditions, heresies, envyings, murders, drunkenness, revellings, and such like: of the which I tell you before, as I have also told you in time past, that they which do such things shall not inherit the kingdom of God.

Now think about it.

Now, when you follow the desires of your sinful nature, the evil results will be obvious and clearly seen by all others. Here they are: adultery (sexual immorality by those who at one time promised faithfulness to their spouse), fornication (impure thoughts and actions), uncleanness (filthy in mind and body), lasciviousness (eager to indulge in and satisfy every evil lust), idolatry (making sex the god that you worship), witchcraft (involvement in satanic and demonic activities that are a part of the mainstream pornographic world found on the Internet), hatred (guilt-driven hatred toward those who bring conviction to your life), variance (quarreling, arguing, and fighting to keep

Fighting to keep control . . . control so that no one can dig up and expose your hidden sin), emulations (jealousy and passionate desire for that which is not yours to have), wrath (fits of rage that often accompany an immoral life that is already out of control in so many other ways), strife (selfish ambitions that push all others aside to enable you to get what you think you have to have), seditions (dissension and division from friends and family members because your habitual sin is more important to you than they are), heresies (you belong to a faction that feels that you alone are right and everyone else is wrong), envyings (nothing is ever enough, and there is always a desire for more), murders (it is hard to believe, but some even resort to murder in order to cover up their sexual sins), drunkenness (if you frequent places where illicit sex is available, there will often be drinking and drunkenness also), revellings (wild parties, orgies, carousing), and many other sins like these: let me warn you again, as I have told you before, that those who are habitually involved in these kinds of sins and lifestyles will not inherit the kingdom of God; they will not spend eternity in heaven.

This is what God says.

1 Corinthians 6:9–11

Know ye not that the unrighteous shall not inherit the kingdom of God? Be not deceived: neither fornicators, nor idolaters, nor adulterers, nor effeminate, nor abusers of themselves with mankind, nor thieves, nor covetous, nor drunkards, nor revilers, nor extortioners, shall inherit the kingdom of God. And such were some of you: but ye are washed, but ye are sanctified, but ye are justified in the name of the Lord Jesus, and by the Spirit of our God.

Now think about it.

Don't you know that those consumed with habitual sin and wickedness will not inherit the kingdom of God? Don't be fooled; do not deceive or trick yourself into thinking something that is simply not true: those who indulge in sexual immorality, who are idolaters worshiping the god of sex, unfaithful adulterers, male prostitutes (effeminate), homosexuals (abusers of themselves with mankind), thieves stealing the purity of others, greedy people (covetous), drunkards, abusive slanderers (revilers), or swindlers (extortioners) will not inherit the kingdom of God. Don't forget, that is exactly what some of you were before you trusted Jesus Christ as your Savior; but now you are washed, you are set apart as a unique and special child of God (sanctified), you are now right with God (justified) because of what the Lord Jesus and God's Holy Spirit did for you.

Meditation 7

Why do you want what God forbids you to have?

This is what God says.

Proverbs 9:13–18

A foolish woman is clamorous: she is simple, and knoweth nothing. For she sitteth at the door of her house, on a seat in the high places of the city, to call passengers who go right on their ways: whoso is simple, let him turn in hither: and as for him that wanteth understanding, she saith to him, Stolen waters are sweet, and bread eaten in secret is pleasant. But he knoweth not that the dead are there; and that her guests are in the depths of hell.

Now think about it.

A foolish, empty, wicked woman loudly tempts weak men whose minds already dwell on sexual sins (just as wicked men tempt weak women); she is simple-minded, naïve, and undisciplined and doesn't even know it. For she sits at her front door on a very high seat in the city, placing herself where she is sure to be seen to tempt anyone who comes her way; whatever guy she can find who is simple, foolish, weak, and controlled by sexual desires, she begs him to go in to her. And as for him that lacks wisdom and understanding, not thinking about the consequences of the choice he is about to make, she says to him, "Stolen waters are sweet (sin is pleasurable for a season, but the seasons end and the sweetness turns to bitterness) and bread eaten in secret (which even though it may be a secret today will not remain a secret tomorrow; it will be found out) is pleasant, at least for a while." But he does not know that all the men who went in to her before him are dead and now in the grave.

How can this affect me?

If a person dwells on sexual fantasies, maybe even rationalizing that he will never really act them out, he is just fooling himself. Those who have started the process in the mind are the "simple" this passage is talking about. They have made up so many "pretend" situations in their mind, that when the first opportunity comes, they fall without a fight. By the way, the opportunities to sin will continue to come because there are many strange men and women on the prowl looking for new conquests. These evil seducers consistently put themselves in places to be seen—commercials, billboards, websites, magazines, beaches, malls, movies, sports events—to entrap the simple-minded. Don't just resist these strange men and women. Run from them!

Meditation 8

The root of all sexual sin is selfish pride!
This is what God says.

Proverbs 16:18

Pride goeth before destruction, and an haughty spirit before a fall.

Now think about it.

Pride, selfishness, and arrogant self-confidence set you up for destruction, and a haughty spirit, a no-one-can-tell-me-I'm-wrong attitude, is in control of your thinking just before you fall into sin.

56

How can this affect me?

What is your attitude toward habitual sin? If you proudly think you not only know when to stop but can stop anytime you choose, you're fooling yourself. If you've got the attitude that you can continue in your sin and no one will ever find out, you're just fooling yourself. If you think you can enjoy your sin and will never experience any consequences for it, get ready for disappointment and destruction. Your reputation will be destroyed. Your relationships will be destroyed. Your confidence will be destroyed. Your walk with God will be destroyed. Those who lift themselves high above God's clear warnings fall so fast and so far down that they hardly ever crawl out of their destruction.

This is what God says.

Proverbs 18:12

Before destruction the heart of man is haughty,
and before honour is humility.

Now think about it.

Before a man's downfall, before his testimony and reputation are totally demolished, his heart is proud; and before a man is honored, praised, and thanked for living an unselfish life that walks with God and is a blessing to others, he exhibits humility, which is an honest appraisal of his worthlessness before God.

How can this affect me?

A proud heart makes you think you can resist sin. You can fight this thing off. You can find total victory in yourself. You have the strength to be in control over your sin. You can win! A humble heart realizes you can't do it. Left to yourself you will be defeated. You alone will be under the control and domination of your sexual sin. You will lose the battle if you don't get help. Which of these two ways do you think? Is your heart proud or humble?

This is what God says.

Proverbs 29:23

A man's pride shall bring him low: but honour shall uphold the humble in spirit.

Now think about it.

A man's selfishness and pride will humiliate him, and his embarrassment will take him lower than he can imagine; but the humble in spirit, those who have an honest attitude about their strengths and weaknesses, will keep their honor and testimony before their family and friends.

How can this affect me?

I have counseled men, former spiritual leaders, who sit in total humiliation and devastation today (and some even in jail) because they "thought" they could handle their sin and get away with it. Sin starts small and rapidly escalates to a place of total shame. These men did not choose to humble themselves; instead, they were "humbled" (losing your ministry and family is very humbling). They thought they could handle it! They couldn't.

This is what God says.

1 Corinthians 10:12

Wherefore let him that thinketh he standeth take heed lest he fall.

Now think about it.

If you *think* you can stand strong in your own strength, if you *think* you can handle it, if you *think* you've got everything under control, if you *think* you can stop your secret sins anytime you want, take heed, watch out, be careful . . . get ready for a big fall.

How can this affect me?

Do you *think* you can handle it on your own? Be careful!

This is what God says.

James 4:6–8

But he giveth more grace. Wherefore he saith, God resisteth the proud, but giveth grace unto the humble. Submit yourselves therefore to God. Resist the devil, and he will flee from you. Draw nigh to God, and he will draw nigh to you. Cleanse your hands, ye sinners; and purify your hearts, ye double minded.

Now think about it.

God gives more and more grace and strength to help us to say no to our evil desires. But He reminds us who He gives this strength to and who He keeps it from. God resists (keeps a distance from) the proud but gives grace to the humble. Stop thinking you are so great and submit yourself to God. (Listen to Him. Obey His Word. Stop sinning! God wants only what is best for you.) Fight off and resist the Devil (your hidden enemy who hates you and wants nothing more than to destroy your relationship with God and others through your sexual sin), and this hateful, proud enemy called the Devil will flee from you. Draw close to God, and He will draw close to you. (We can be just as close to God as we want to be!) How? Those of you who are living in sin (you sinners), clean up your life, get rid of everything that makes it easy for you to sin, whether it is ungodly associates or unfiltered Internet access; and you double-minded hypocrites (fakes, phonies, pretending that everything is fine between you and God while you are secretly living in sexual sin), purify your hearts by asking for God's undeserved forgiveness.

How can this affect me?

You can choose to proudly fight your evil desires in your own strength without God's grace and help, or you can choose to humbly admit your own weakness and fight with the power of an almighty, all-powerful God.

C. H. Spurgeon said, "Pride is so natural to fallen man that it springs up in his heart like weeds in a watered garden, or rushes by a flowing brook. It is an all pervading sin, and smothers all things like dust in the roads, or flour in the mill. Its every touch is evil. You may hunt down this fox, and think you have destroyed it, and lo! Your very exultation is pride. None have more pride than those who dream that they have none. Pride is a sin with a thousand lives; it seems impossible to kill it."

"Pride was the sin that turned Satan, a blessed angel, into a cursed devil. Satan knows better than anyone the damning power of pride. Is it any wonder, then, that he so often uses it to poison the saints? His design is made easier in that man's heart shows a natural fondness for it. Pride, like liquor, is intoxicating. A swallow or two usually leaves a man worthless to God," said William Gurnall, seventeenth-century Puritan writer.

Meditation 9

Don't be fooled by flattery (she really does not want you).

This is what God says.

Proverbs 6:24–29

To keep thee from the evil woman, from the flattery of the tongue of a strange woman. Lust not after her beauty in thine heart; neither let her take thee with her eyelids. For by means of a whorish woman a man is brought to a piece of bread: and the adulteress will hunt for the precious life. Can a man take fire in his bosom, and his clothes not be burned? Can one go upon hot coals, and

63

his feet not be burned? So he that goeth in to his neighbour's wife; whosoever toucheth her shall not be innocent.

Now think about it.

Obedience to God's simple commands will keep or guard you from all evil women (and evil men), whether you see them at work, in a magazine, in a movie, or on a website and from the flattery of the tongue of a strange woman, which is nothing but lies. These wicked seducers don't really want you and they are certainly not attracted to you physically. You're just another toy in their toy box to play with and then throw away. Don't believe their smooth talk and flattery; they want your money and a good laugh, nothing more. You mean absolutely nothing to them. Do not lust after their beauty in your heart; don't let your intense passions and desires totally control your heart and mind; neither allow them to allure you, captivate you, or seduce you by the way you "think" they are looking at you. It's all fake! It is a game they are playing. The tempter and temptress, whether in print or real life, simply want to prove that they are stronger than you.

By the way, if you choose to chase after these immoral men and women, it will cost you more than you know, for prostitutes and pornography will rob you blind and bring you to poverty. If you follow this lifestyle to the end, you will lose everything but maybe a crusty old piece of bread to eat. Seeking sexual pleasure from another man's wife (the adulteress) or another woman's husband not only will destroy your testimony, your trust, and your confidence, but it could cost you your life. You play with fire, you will get burned. Can a man take fire in his bosom, and his clothes not be burned?

You cannot choose the consequences of your sin.

Can one go upon hot coals, and his feet not be burned? There is no way you can get away with habitual sexual sin whether it is through television, prostitutes, pornography, or even willing individuals. You can choose your sin but you cannot choose the consequences of your sin. This is what will happen to anyone who seeks to be satisfied sexually by anyone other than his or her own spouse. Don't touch! Don't touch another man's wife. Don't touch another woman's husband. Don't touch the magazine by picking it up and leafing through it. Don't touch the video or DVD. Don't touch the computer mouse that will click your way to someone who is not *your* wife or not *your* husband. Whoever touches them will not be innocent or go unpunished. Sexual sin will cost you everything you have.

How can this affect me?

Let's not be fooled into thinking these wicked men and women really want us. They don't. Men, do not let another man's wife overpower you by the way she acts or looks. Stay away from her. Don't look at her. Don't touch her. Ladies, do not let any man other than your husband or future husband flatter you. Stay away from him. Don't look at him. Don't touch him. Promise God you will not "touch" a piece of pornography. Promise God you will not "touch" (in a suggestive, tantalizing way) anyone other than your spouse. It will destroy everything you ever wish to be.

Meditation 10

Whom are you trying to fool anyway?
This is what God says.

Luke 11:39–40

And the Lord said unto him, Now do ye Pharisees
make clean the outside of the cup and the platter;
but your inward part is full of ravening and wickedness. Ye fools, did not he that made that which
is without make that which is within also?

Now think about it.

And the Lord said unto him, You Pharisees are careful to clean the outside of the cup and the dish; you do all you can to keep your appearance up before your family and friends because you do not want them to know what is really going on inside, that you really are filthy and full of greed and wickedness, desiring that which is not yours to have and wickedly seeking to pursue it. You fools, don't you realize that God made both the outside and the inside, and He knows what is going on in both areas?

How can this affect me?

Don't be so consumed with keeping your sin hidden and covering your selfish, sensual habits that you fail to deal with the root problems of your selfishness. Just because you look squeaky clean on the outside does not mean that greed and lust are not growing like cancer on your inside. Your selfishness proves that you have a wrong focus. Your greed reveals you have a discontented heart. Your lust simply shows who and what you truly love. Deep down inside, you love yourself. All change needs to come from the inside out.

This is what God says.

1 Peter 3:3–4

Whose adorning let it not be that outward adorning of plaiting the hair, and of wearing of gold, or of putting on of apparel; but let it be the hidden man of the heart, in that which is not corruptible, even the ornament of a meek and quiet spirit, which is in the sight of God of great price.

Now think about it.

Men, don't be consumed with women or girls who are consumed with what they look like. And, ladies, don't be consumed with your outward appearance (outward adorning), those who give undue attention to the way they wear their hair (plaiting the hair), those who try to catch someone's eye by flaunting expensive jewelry (wearing of gold), or those who love to wear the popular yet immodest styles of the world by choosing clothes that are too tight, too low, or too short and draw attention away from the face (putting on of apparel). But let it be the hidden man of the heart, the character, the personality, the real person that is on the inside that attracts you, the unfading, incorruptible beauty of a gentle and quiet spirit,

69

which is in the sight of God precious and priceless and should be the same in our sight.

How can this affect me?

Hey, guys, if you are living a phony life that appears to be great on the outside but is filthy on the inside, you will be attracted to girls who are also attractive on the outside but filthy on the inside. Ladies, does that describe you? Men, what kind of girl attracts your eye? What is she communicating with the way she carries herself and what she wears (or does not wear) that would make you want to spend time with her? Is she the kind of girl you want for a wife? A daughter? A wife for your son? Would she help raise children to have hearts for God that are pure, gentle, and loving? Would God see her character as precious? Remember, every girl involved in pornography is somebody's wife or daughter and will someday stand before God for her actions. She is a real person that needs God to free her from the bondage of her own sexual sin. Men, don't be consumed with such a girl. And, please, girls, moms, daughters, wives . . . don't become that kind of girl.

This is what God says.

1 Samuel 16:7

But the Lord said unto Samuel, Look not on his countenance, or on the height of his stature; because I have refused him: for the Lord seeth not as man seeth; for man looketh on the outward appearance, but the Lord looketh on the heart.

Now think about it.

But the Lord said unto Samuel, "Don't judge or consider his appearance or height. Just because everything looks great on the outside does not mean that it is great on the inside. Even though things look fine to everyone around, I cannot use him. For I am the Lord and I cannot be fooled like man can; I do not see things the same way a man sees them; I know what is going on in his private life." Most spouses, parents, and friends look only on the exterior and can be fooled, but the Lord looks on the heart and sees the thoughts, the desires, and the intentions.

How can this affect me?

You can fool some of the people all the time, and all the people some of the time, but you cannot fool God anytime. Just because you are in a Christian leadership position, just because you have gifts to teach, preach, sing, or lead, just because you have a "name" or a reputation, just because most people think you would never be involved in habitual sexual sins, just because you can fool many people, you still cannot fool God. If you think you can fool God, you are just fooling yourself. God sees and knows exactly what is going on inside of you.

This is what God says.

1 John 1:6–10

If we say that we have fellowship with him, and walk in darkness, we lie, and do not the truth: but if we walk in the light, as he is in the light, we have fellowship one with another, and the blood of Jesus Christ his Son cleanseth us from all sin. If we say that we have no sin, we deceive ourselves, and the truth is not in us. If we confess our sins, he is faithful and just to forgive us our sins, and to cleanse us from all unrighteousness. If we say that we have not sinned, we make him a liar, and his word is not in us.

Now think about it.

If we say that we have fellowship with God, we say that we are close to the Lord, we say that we have our little struggles now and then but are doing okay, and continually walk in the darkness of habitual sexual sin, we are bold-faced liars and are not practicing or living in the truth; but if we walk in the light just like Jesus does, if we live in the light of God's presence the same way Jesus Christ does, then we can have fellowship with each other. We do not have to deceitfully cover and hide our private lives but can have totally open and accountable relationships with our spouses and friends. And remember, the blood of Jesus Christ, God's Son, cleanses us from all sin so that we can have that fellowship with God that He desires and we should strive for. If we say that we have no sin, but are living a secret life of habitual sexual sin, we are simply lying to ourselves and fooling ourselves and are refusing to

If we confess our sins . . .

accept the truth that we are in big trouble. If we confess our sins, and agree with God that our selfish fantasies, our uncontrolled and filthy minds are wicked, evil, and despicable, God will forgive us! He is faithful and just to forgive us our sins, and to cleanse us from all unrighteousness . . . yes, every evil thought, evil desire, and evil action. By the way, if we deny that we have a problem, saying it really is not sin by justifying it in a hundred different ways, if we say that we have not sinned, we are actually calling God a liar and proving that His Word has no place in our lives.

How can this affect me?

We can lie to others but not to ourselves ... and never to God. We are fooling ourselves if we live in continuous, habitual sexual sin and say we are walking with God on a daily basis. Decide in your heart to do away with your self-deception. Stop deceiving others. There is hope if you admit the truth about your sin and your relationship with God. Even though God knows your present condition, He still wants to forgive you. He wants to cleanse you! He wants to renew that close fellowship you once had.

Meditation 11

Everything you say can and will be used against you!

This is what God says.

Proverbs 12:13

The wicked is snared by the transgression of his lips: but the just shall come out of trouble.

Now think about it.

A wicked, evil, sinful man is trapped or snared by his own filthy mouth and suggestive talking, but the godly man who seeks to do right, who refuses to talk filthy in order to entice or seduce someone else, will escape the troublesome consequences of sin.

How can this affect me?

Your lips and tongue are the tattletale of your heart. If you talk filthy, you have a filthy heart. It is far too easy today for our tongues to get us into serious trouble with sexual sins. The tongue often lights the fuse that results in an explosion of sexual sin. For some, it may be as simple as a flirtatious comment on how nice someone looks at work or school. For others, it could be a call to a "900" number. Still others choose to be involved in sexually arousing chatter that takes place online in adult-oriented chatrooms. Your tongue can get you into big trouble. Refuse to be suggestive in your communication with others. Refuse to talk dirty to anyone, anywhere or anytime. Refuse to hang around others who get their sexual thrills with foolish conversation. Pray like the psalmist in Psalm 101:3–4, "Set a watch, O Lord, before my mouth; keep the door of my lips. Incline not my heart to any evil thing, to practise wicked works with men that work iniquity." Be careful what you say . . . everything you say can and will be used against you.

This is what God says.

Matthew 12:34–35

O generation of vipers, how can ye, being evil, speak good things? for out of the abundance of the heart the mouth speaketh. A good man out of the good treasure of the heart bringeth forth good things: and an evil man out of the evil treasure bringeth forth evil things.

Now think about it.

You brood of forked-tongued snakes, how can you speak all these good things when you've got such wicked, evil hearts? You say only what you think, feel, and believe in your hearts. Good men, out of good hearts, say good things: evil, wicked men, out of evil, wicked hearts, say evil, wicked things.

This is what God says.

Matthew 15:18–20

But those things which proceed out of the mouth come forth from the heart; and they defile the man. For out of the heart proceed evil thoughts, murders, adulteries, fornications, thefts, false witness, blasphemies: these are the things which defile a man: but to eat with unwashen hands defileth not a man.

Now think about it.

What you say comes directly from the heart; it is those thoughts that defile you. It is from your heart that come evil thoughts, hate-motivated murders, habitual sexual sins such as adultery, premarital sex, and pornography, stealing (not just things, but the purity and innocence of others), constant lying, and slander to cover up your secret sins. These are the things which defile a man and make you filthy inside; eating with unwashed hands will not defile you and make you unacceptable to God.

How can this affect me?

Listen to what you are saying. Is it easy for you to talk openly about your sexual desires? Do you look for ways to verbalize your wicked cravings? Do you actively seek to talk about sexual matters in adult chat rooms? If you do, it should scare you to death. Do not fool yourself into thinking that it is not "as bad" to talk about it as to actually do it! Those addicted to sexual sin follow a dangerous three-step process:

Think about it . . .

Talk about it . . .

Do it.

Sexual addiction is a heart issue. What you say simply reveals what you are. Again, what you say can and will be used against you.

Meditation 12

Be careful whom you listen to!
This is what God says.

Matthew 15:14

Let them alone: they be blind leaders of the blind.
And if the blind lead the blind, both shall fall into
the ditch.

Now think about it.

Just ignore those who ignore God's Word and justify
sin: they are blind guides trying to lead blind people. If
one blind person leads another blind person, they both
are going to fall into a ditch.

How can this affect me?

Do not listen to anyone who justifies sexual sin! It is not just a phase of life men go through. It is not just a natural way to express love. It is not okay as long as no one gets hurt or pregnant or contracts a sexually transmitted disease. It is not justified just because two consenting adults are involved. There is no "soft" porn that is fine to view. There are no sexual activities you can engage in with others just as long as you do not "go all the way." Sex is not dirty. Sex is for marriage between one man and one woman. Anyone who teaches that any sexual activity and fulfillment outside of marriage is fine (whether it is virtual or real) is blind and cannot clearly see what God's Word has to say about purity and sexuality. If you follow a blind leader who justifies sexual sin in any way, you will end up in a ditch with him. And remember, some ditches are so deep you may never be able to crawl out.

This is what God says.

1 Peter 4:3–5

For the time past of our life may suffice us to have wrought the will of the Gentiles, when we walked

81

in lasciviousness, lusts, excess of wine, revellings, banquetings, and abominable idolatries: wherein they think it strange that ye run not with them to the same excess of riot, speaking evil of you: who shall give account to him that is ready to judge the quick and the dead.

Now think about it.

We have spent enough of our past lifetime trying to please and be accepted by godless unbelievers by doing the evil things that they enjoy—they lived lives that were lewd and morally out of control, feeding their flesh and lustful desires with every sexual perversion imaginable. Nothing was off-limits to them even if it meant the exploitation of children and women. They were exceedingly sinful in their drunkenness, gluttony, orgies, carousing, wild parties (wine, revellings, banquetings), and detestable idolatries, which also involved sexual immorality even in the way they worshiped. You must realize that your former friends who are unsaved think it's strange that you quit running with them and no longer join their wild parties or get involved in their sin and immorality, speaking evil of you, making fun of you, mocking and abusing you in an attempt to shame you back into your former lifestyle; but keep in mind, these former friends will have to personally face God and give an account directly to Him, and He will judge them like He is going to judge all men, both the living and the dead.

How can this affect me?

Many individuals addicted and enslaved to sexual sins enjoy the company of other addicts. For some reason, the idea that "everybody is doing it" seems to justify sin and soften the guilt. We are warned that evil, wicked friends and companions corrupt good morals. The peer pressure from those who live in constant immorality is almost irresistible because they are coaxing you to do something your flesh wants to do anyway. Run from those friends. You owe them absolutely nothing. And remember, the pornographers, the movie writers, and those who make it a game to steal someone's virginity will all stand before God, face to face, and will regret the choices they made and the fact that they ruined so many other lives.

Meditation 13

You can't beat this all by yourself.
This is what God says.

Ecclesiastes 4:9–12

Two are better than one; because they have a good reward for their labour. For if they fall, the one will lift up his fellow: but woe to him that is alone when he falleth; for he hath not another to help him up. Again, if two lie together, then they have heat: but how can one be warm alone? And if one prevail against him, two shall withstand him; and a threefold cord is not quickly broken.

Now think about it.

If you daily face uncontrollable sinful desires, it is good to have a friend who will help you because two are better than one; they can accomplish so much more than one who tries to work this out on his own. If you have confided in a friend who walks with God and experiences consistent victory over sexual temptations and you in your weakness again fall into sexual sin, your friend will help you to admit your sin, confess it, and spiritually get you back up on your feet. But I feel sorry for the person who struggles with habitual sexual sin and is all alone when he falls; for there is no one there to help him up. To illustrate this principle better, on a very cold night, if two are under the same blanket, they can warm each other up, but isn't it hard to get warm when you are all alone? And if someone is attacked, two can defend themselves much better than one. They can stand back and fight the enemy from every direction. And even better, a rope made of three cords is not easily broken.

How can this affect me?

You can't win this struggle on your own.

You need a friend . . .

- that you can daily confide in and be accountable to.
- that will check up on you to see what kind of decisions you are making.
- that will confront you when you are in sin.
- that will hate your sin and love you.
- that will care enough to make life miserable for you until you see your foolishness and turn from your habitual sin to God.

Until you confess your sin and share your struggle with someone, you will continue to struggle. The simple fact that someone else knows and is watching out for you is a great motivation to change. Get a good friend who really cares about you and share your heart with him. The two of you can fight off the enemy from every side.

Meditation 14

You are accountable to God Himself!
This is what God says.

Romans 14:12

So then every one of us shall give account of himself to God.

Now think about it.

Yes, it is a sure thing that each one of us will give a
personal account of himself to God.

How can this affect me?

When we talk about an accountability partner, I think we often forget that technically, every individual on earth already has an all-knowing, all-powerful accountability partner. He is God! A true accountability partner insists that we honestly share with him what is going on in our lives. Someday, you will give an account to God of what you have done, what you have thought, what sins you have refused to forsake, and most of all, what you have done in regard to trusting or rejecting Jesus Christ as your Savior and Lord. Everyone will bow before God as sovereign Ruler and King; everyone will give an "account" of choices he or she has made. God is the ultimate accountability partner.

This is what God says.

1 Corinthians 3:16–18

Know ye not that ye are the temple of God, and that the Spirit of God dwelleth in you? If any man defile the temple of God, him shall God destroy; for the temple of God is holy, which temple ye are. Let no man deceive himself. If any man among you seemeth to be wise in this world, let him become a fool, that he may be wise.

Now think about it.

Don't you know and realize that you are the temple of God and that the Spirit of God dwells in you? If you defile or destroy the temple of God by bringing in worship to your gods of sensuality, God will destroy you in His way and His time; for God's temple (that's you) is to be sacred, special, holy, and unlike all others. Don't fool or deceive yourself and justify your habitual sexual sin by thinking that it is no big deal to God and that He does not really care so much about His temple . . . He does. So stop fooling yourself. If you think you have it all together and are wise according to the world's standards, you had better back up and take a closer look at how foolish you are according to God's standards.

How can this affect me?

This passage helps us to understand that we really are quite foolish and know much less than we think we know. Paul emphasized, "Don't you know?" "Don't deceive yourself!" "If you think you are so wise, you had better look again." God promises to judge those who defile, ruin, and destroy His temple. Both the tabernacle and the temple of Bible times were constructed in such a way as to force people to focus on Jehovah God. Both the tabernacle and the temple were protected from all impurities and defilement. If an unbeliever closely examined your "temple," what would he think of your God? Don't be fooled. Don't be deceived. What you do with your body does matter.

Meditation 15

Sin can be resisted. Sin must be resisted!
This is what God says.

Romans 6:12–14

Let not sin therefore reign in your mortal body, that ye should obey it in the lusts thereof. Neither yield ye your members as instruments of unrighteousness unto sin: but yield yourselves unto God, as those that are alive from the dead, and your members as instruments of righteousness unto God. For sin shall not have dominion over you: for ye are not under the law, but under grace.

Now think about it.

Do not let sin control the way you live. Do not give in to the selfish and sensual desires of your mortal body. Do not obey your ever-demanding flesh as if it were your master or king. Neither yield to, give in to, surrender to, or admit defeat to your body or any member of your body. Do not let any part of your body, not any part at all, be used for selfish, sinful sexual satisfaction; but instead give God total control and yield yourselves to God. If you are a Christian, God has given you a brand new life, just as though you had died and then were raised from the dead. Use your body as a tool in the hands of a mighty God to do good and not evil. For sin shall not have dominion over you: sin does not need to be in control. You are under no obligation to obey your flesh. The sinful desires you face daily are not your master or king. Stop giving in to them, for you are not under the law, but under grace.

How can this affect me?

You have a choice. You have been given the ability and free will to choose who and what will be the king in your life. You choose who and what will be in control. You choose who and what you will obey. You choose to whom and to what you will yield. You choose who and what will dominate your life. You choose to please God or please self. You choose.

This is what God says.

Romans 6:16

Know ye not, that to whom ye yield yourselves servants to obey, his servants ye are to whom ye obey; whether of sin unto death, or of obedience unto righteousness?

Now think about it.

Don't you know, don't you realize, has this never dawned on you, that whatever you choose to obey becomes your master and you become its servant or slave? If you choose sin (whether it's a wicked thought life or actual sexual misconduct) as your master, you will receive the incredible consequences of your sin that could lead to death. If God is your choice as Master, you will receive God's approval for your self-controlled, righteous (right) actions.

How can this affect me?

We will always have to battle the powerful presence of sin in our lives, but once the Spirit of God enters our hearts, sin is no longer in charge. Sin is no longer our master or boss. Sin can be resisted. Sin must be resisted! God's Spirit can empower you to refuse sin's domination of your life, but it is your choice. You choose who is your master! Don't yield. Don't give up or surrender to sin. Be a servant of God and not a slave to sin.

This is what God says.

Ephesians 4:17–19

This I say therefore, and testify in the Lord, that ye henceforth walk not as other Gentiles walk, in the vanity of their mind, having the understanding darkened, being alienated from the life of God through the ignorance that is in them, because of the blindness of their heart: who being past feeling have given themselves over unto lasciviousness, to work all uncleanness with greediness.

Now think about it.

In order to live in victory over habitual sexual sin, this is what you need to know, and I say it with the Lord's authority. Now that you are a believer and know Christ personally, from this point on do not live like the ungodly unbelievers, with foolish, empty, and confused minds, having their understanding darkened and their minds closed, being alienated and separated from the life of God because of the ignorance that is in them because they choose to harden their hearts in order to keep their sin. Their hearts are so past feeling, hardened, and calloused that they have totally given in to an uncontrolled life of immorality and filthiness. They have an intense, greedy desire to satisfy themselves with sexual thoughts and immoral activities. God is so grieved when believers, those who know better, live and walk as if they never knew God existed, like a complete unbeliever.

How can this affect me?

If you want to live a life consumed with sensual desires, the same kind of life lived by an unsaved person who does not know God, let your evil thoughts callous your heart. Habitual sexual sin will ultimately desensitize your heart in such a way you will lose all feeling. Guilt and conviction will no longer have the effect they used to. You will not repent. You will not even want to.

Meditation 16

Don't just stay away from sin.
Stay away from temptation!
This is what God says.

Matthew 5:27–30

Ye have heard that it was said by them of old time, Thou shalt not commit adultery: but I say unto you, That whosoever looketh on a woman to lust after her hath committed adultery with her already in his heart. And if thy right eye offend thee, pluck it out, and cast it from thee: for it is profitable for thee that one of thy members should perish, and not that thy whole body should be cast into hell.

And if thy right hand offend thee, cut it off, and cast it from thee: for it is profitable for thee that one of thy members should perish, and not that thy whole body should be cast into hell.

Now think about it.

You have heard and know that one of the Ten Commandments says, Thou shalt not commit adultery; but Jesus tells us, you and me, that anyone who looks at a woman lustfully (desiring to be sexually involved with her) has already committed adultery with her in his heart. If your right eye causes you to sin, gouge it out and throw it away: it would be better for you to lose an eye than for your whole body to be thrown into hell for eternity. And if your right hand (your strongest hand) causes you to sin, cut it off and throw it away: it would be better for you to lose your right hand than for your whole body to be thrown into hell for eternity.

How can this affect me?

In this passage, the Lord is not advocating any type of self-mutilation. He is showing the seriousness of the consequences of sin. Those who choose their sin over God, those who have decided that they will live their lives any way they want, those who would rather satisfy their fleshly desires with immorality and sensuality than to admit that they are sinners deserving of the wrath of God would be better off gouging out their eyes and cutting off their right hand than spending eternity in hell. A few short years of sensual pleasure does not compare with eternity separated from God. Cut it out or cut it off. What area of your life needs some radical amputation? Do you need to cut out all TV? Do you need to eliminate the Internet from your life? Do you need to cut off old friendships? Do you need to cut up all credit cards and ATM cards so that you cannot purchase your sin? What needs to be cut off or cut out of your life? I think you already know, so cut it out now!

This is what God says.

2 Corinthians 6:14–7:1

Be ye not unequally yoked together with unbe-lievers: for what fellowship hath righteousness with unrighteousness? and what communion hath light with darkness? And what concord

99

hath Christ with Belial? or what part hath he that believeth with an infidel? And what agreement hath the temple of God with idols? for ye are the temple of the living God; as God hath said, I will dwell in them, and walk in them; and I will be their God, and they shall be my people. Wherefore come out from among them, and be ye separate, saith the Lord, and touch not the unclean thing; and I will receive you, and will be a Father unto you, and ye shall be my sons and daughters, saith the Lord Almighty. Having therefore these promises, dearly beloved, let us cleanse ourselves from all filthiness of the flesh and spirit, perfecting holiness in the fear of God.

Now think about it.

Don't yoke or team up with unbelievers. For what do righteousness and wickedness have in common? How can light and darkness live with each other? What togetherness, camaraderie, and harmony can Christ have with the worthless Devil himself? What do a believer and an unbelieving infidel have in common? (How can you spend hours surrounding yourself with unbelieving sexual perverts, whether on screen or in person, and say that you have a relationship with God?) How can there be any agreement between worshiping God in His temple and worshiping idols? If you are a Christian, did you forget that you are the temple of the living God (the Holy Spirit of God dwells within you)? God has said, I will dwell in them, and walk in them; and I will be their God, and they shall be My people. Because we as believers have the Spirit of God living within us, we must come out from among them and separate ourselves from those who not only are addicted to sex themselves but do everything they can to keep us addicted also. The Lord also says, "Don't touch their unclean, filthy things!" (Refuse to touch anything associated with immorality. Refuse to touch a magazine. Refuse to touch a mouse or keypad that will send you to the dark world of pornography. Refuse to touch another man's wife or any woman who is not your wife. Refuse to touch another woman's husband or even a single man. God says, "Don't touch! Keep your hands off!") Then the Lord Almighty said, "I will receive you and will be a Father to you, and you will be My sons and daughters.

God has said, I will dwell in them . . .

(I want to have a close, family relationship with you. But I cannot if you continue to associate with wicked people who are involved in such sexual perversions.)" My dearly loved friends, since we have these promises, the promises of a close, personal relationship with God Himself, let's cleanse ourselves from all filthiness (all sexual sin whether in mind or action) and everything that can defile our bodies and spirit. And we should work toward complete purity and mature holiness as we learn to live in the fear of God (a constant awareness of God's presence and power combined with a wholesome dread of displeasing Him).

How can this affect me?

The proper question in regard to personal purity is not "How far can I go?" but "How pure can I be?" Those who insist on living on the edge are precariously close to falling over the edge. It is a life of fear. Fear that someone will see you. Fear that you will get caught. Fear that you might go "too far" and not be able to come back. Fear that God wants nothing to do with you. Fear that you may not really be saved. Fear that you might fall. Stay away from the edge. Stay away from sin by staying away from temptation. Separate yourself from all ungodly influences in person, on screen, or in print. Come out from among wicked people. Separate yourself from all evil influence. Stay away from sin!

This is what God says.

Proverbs 5:3–13

For the lips of a strange woman drop as an honeycomb, and her mouth is smoother than oil: but her end is bitter as wormwood, sharp as a twoedged sword. Her feet go down to death; her steps take hold on hell. Lest thou shouldest ponder the path of life, her ways are moveable, that thou canst not know them. Hear me now therefore, O ye children, and depart not from the words of my mouth. Remove thy way far from her, and come not nigh the door of her house: lest thou give thine honour unto others, and thy years unto the cruel: lest strangers be filled with thy wealth; and thy labours be in the house of a stranger; and thou mourn at the last, when thy flesh and thy body are consumed, and say, How have I hated instruction, and my heart despised reproof; and have not obeyed the voice of my teachers, nor inclined mine ear to them that instructed me!

Now think about it.

The lips of an immoral woman (or an immoral man) are sweet as honey and as enjoyable as a delicious piece of candy, and she is a smooth talker, smoother than oil, but in the end, she is as bitter as poison, sharp as a twoedged sword (both of which will easily destroy you). Her feet go down to death; her steps lead straight to the grave; she will kill your testimony, she will kill your purity, she will kill your confidence, she will kill your relationship with God and others, and she will kill you. Lest you should even think about following her lifestyle, her ways are very unstable; you have no idea what you are getting into. Therefore, listen to me carefully, my children, and do not turn or forget what I am about to say to you. Run from her! Don't even walk on the same sidewalk or path she uses. Stay away from the door of her house; stay so far away you forget where it is, lest you lose your honorable testimony and reputation and hand all your life's achievements to wicked, uncaring people. Lest you blow all your hard-earned savings and money on sexual sins, giving all you have earned to people you do not know, and your years of hard work and labor you squander to a bunch of immoral people who couldn't care less about you. And you finally mourn, weep, and cry because you have thrown everything good and important away to immoral people and all you have left is the heartache and the sexually transmitted diseases associated with a life of promiscuity, and you finally say, it is all my fault. But it is too late now. Why did I hate clear, Bible instruction, and why did my heart despise reproof? Why did I demand my own way? Oh, why didn't I listen to my teachers? Why didn't I listen closely to those who instructed me and tried to help me? Why? Why? Why?

How can this affect me?

Run from sexual sins! Stay away from all the temptations you can! Get away as fast and as far as you possibly can! Do not waste years of peace, joy, and happiness for a few hours of sexual pleasure. Run now so that you will not end your life crying out to God, "Why? Why? Why?"

Just a reminder—don't just stay away from sin; stay away from temptation!

Meditation 17

Your thoughts are an index to your character.
This is what God says.

Philippians 4:8

Finally, brethren, whatsoever things are true, whatsoever things are honest, whatsoever things are just, whatsoever things are pure, whatsoever things are lovely, whatsoever things are of good report; if there be any virtue, and if there be any praise, think on these things.

Now think about it.

Finally, my dear brothers and sisters, as I get close to the end of this letter, this is what I want you to think about: whatever things are true, honorable, and right; whatever things are pure, lovely, and admired by others; whatever things are virtuous and praiseworthy. These are the things you need to fix your attention on. Refuse to think and concentrate on anything else.

How can this affect me?

Your reputation is what men think about you, but your character is what God knows about you. Would your reputation be ruined if others knew every little detail of your thought life? Would your closest friends or family members be shocked if they knew what you were thinking each day? What they would find out is what God already knows! Some have reputations that are squeaky clean but characters that are filthy dirty. God gives us a checklist to evaluate our thinking. Is it true? Check. Is it honest? Check. Is it right? Check. Is it pure? Ah, I'm not sure but let's go on. Is it lovely? Well, not really. Is it admired by others? Definitely not. Then stop! Quit thinking about it!

Do you really want everyone to know what God already knows about you? Think about it.

This is what God says.

2 Corinthians 10:5

Casting down imaginations, and every high thing that exalteth itself against the knowledge of God, and bringing into captivity every thought to the obedience of Christ.

Now think about it.

We must cast down, destroy, and demolish every fantasy, imagination, argument, barrier, or proud thought that keeps us away from knowing God (every wicked, selfish thought we choose to think about even though it goes against what we know about God), and we must conquer, capture, and imprison every thought to the obedience of Christ, who should be the center of our thoughts in the first place.

How can this affect me?

We are what we think! What we are thinking today we are becoming tomorrow! Our thoughts truly are an index to our character. We may try to hide, disguise, ignore, or justify selfish thinking, but we are fooling ourselves if we think we can concentrate on wicked thoughts without having our thinking affect our walk with God. We often try to departmentalize our thoughts without making Christ part of that department. Wicked thoughts are garbage that must be thrown or "cast" away. Wicked thinking is imagining sin that we would never want to be caught in. Fantasy thinking is a type of secret virtual reality that someday will become visible reality for all to see. Would you be humiliated or devastated if those closest to you knew everything you were thinking? Who are we actually sinning against when we refuse to capture runaway thoughts? Would you agree that wicked thoughts are actually selfish, defiant acts of disobedience against Jesus Christ Himself? I think it is time for all of us to throw away the trash and clean up our thought lives.

Meditation 18

How can I change? How can I quit?
1. Stay away from temptation!
This is what God says.

Romans 13:13–14

Let us walk honestly, as in the day; not in rioting and drunkenness, not in chambering and wantonness, not in strife and envying. But put ye on the Lord Jesus Christ, and make not provision for the flesh, to fulfil the lusts thereof.

Now think about it.

Let us behave in a proper and decent way as in the daytime when everyone can clearly see and approve of what we are doing. Don't live in darkness, trying to get away with sin just because you think no one can see you. Don't get involved with rioting (wild parties and orgies). Simply refuse to get drunk (which often leads to immorality because your defenses are drowned by the alcohol). Don't live your life in chambering (lewdness, adultery, sexual promiscuity) and wantonness (lust, immoral living, sensuality), not in strife (fighting) and envy (jealousy). Rather than living as a weak man addicted and enslaved to sexual fantasies, put on the pure, holy, decent, and godly characteristics of our Lord Jesus Christ, and do not make it easy to sin by thinking of ways to gratify the flesh and indulge in evil desires.

How can this affect me?

It is much easier to keep away from temptation than it is to keep away from sin. Those who struggle with sexual addiction on any level cannot seem to turn away from the magazine, website, or cable station. But if they never go into the bookstore, stop surfing the web, and get rid of their television, they have a much better chance of staying away from giving in to their evil desires. Make it hard to sin and easy to do right. Our sanctification and holiness dictate that we stay separate from defilements. Separate yourself from the wrong friends, the wrong entertainments, the wrong media, the wrong vacation spots, the wrong movies, the wrong reading material, the wrong websites . . . the wrong! Make it easy to do right by finding friends and activities that strive to exemplify the godly and pure characteristics of our Lord Himself. Be holy, for He is holy.

2. Insulate yourself from evil men and women with the very words of God!
This is what God says.

Proverbs 6:20–24

My son, keep thy father's commandment, and forsake not the law of thy mother: bind them continually upon thine heart, and tie them about thy neck. When thou goest, it shall lead thee; when thou sleepest, it shall keep thee; and when thou awakest, it shall talk with thee. For the commandment is a lamp; and the law is light; and reproofs of instruction are the way of life: to keep thee from the evil woman, from the flattery of the tongue of a strange woman.

Now think about it.

My son, keep your godly father's commandments (guard them so that no one can take them away; keep them in a safe, hidden place where they can never be stolen from you), and do not reject everything your mother has taught you. Do not throw away the simple Bible truths she has tried to pour into your heart. Strongly attach (bind) these Bible truths to your heart and tie them around your neck through memorization and meditation, make the very words of God such an integral part of your heart that they affect the way you think and feel. (Do whatever is necessary to constantly remind yourself of God's Word . . . especially when you are face to face with a life-dominating temptation.) Wherever you go and whatever you do in life, their counsel will lead you; when you sleep, they will keep, guard, and protect you;

each morning when you wake up, God will use His Word to encourage and advise you. For God's commandments and laws are like a bright flashlight clearly showing you your next step in life; and this is the way we should live. Listen to and submit to God's reproof, correction, and discipline that comes from His Word. Here is the blessed result of keeping, guarding, hiding, and acknowledging God's Word in your heart and life; it will keep you, guard you, and protect you from falling prey to evil, immoral women, from the smooth talking and persuasive seduction of all immoral women.

How can this affect me?

God's Word is the answer to consistent victory over habitual sexual sin. It warns us of what we should not do, it tells us how we should think differently, and it encourages us to start doing right. God's Word can and will change us if we follow the Ephesians 4:22–24 method of biblical change: Put off! Put in! Put on! Begin by putting off (stopping) the old, ungodly sinful habits. Through memorization and meditation, put into your mind the scriptural truths that will renew your mind and totally change the way you think. (Wouldn't it be great to have a God-pleasing thought life rather than the one most people wrestle with?) Put on new godly habits. Be obedient to what God says. Keep busy! Keep so busy serving God and others you don't have time to sin.

3. Walk in the Spirit!
This is what God says.
Galatians 5:16–17, 25

This I say then, Walk in the Spirit, and ye shall not fulfil the lust of the flesh. For the flesh lusteth against the Spirit, and the Spirit against the flesh: and these are contrary the one to the other: so that ye cannot do the things that ye would. . . . If we live in the Spirit, let us also walk in the Spirit.

Now think about it.

I say then, Walk in the Spirit, and you will not gratify the evil desires of your sinful flesh. (Just like you trusted Christ for salvation, trust God to lead, guide, and strengthen you to take each step in life in obedience to what He tells you in His Word.) Now you must realize that the old sinful nature desires what is contrary to the Holy Spirit, and the Holy Spirit desires what is contrary to the old sinful nature. (Your sinful nature loves to do evil, which is just the opposite of what the Spirit wants.) They are constantly fighting each other, and you can never do what you should do without conflict. Since you are a believer living in the Spirit and the Spirit of God lives within you, walk in the Spirit. Take every step in purity and holiness, not in your own strength, but by faith, trusting God and obeying Him for the wisdom and strength for each step of obedience.

How can this affect me?

You cannot beat this thing in your own strength. You already know that; you have tried and it doesn't work. Your total dependence on God for salvation needs to be transferred to your daily walk with God. When you trusted Christ as your Savior, do you remember praying something like "Lord, I cannot save myself. I am too wicked and too weak. I trust You, and You alone, to forgive me and cleanse me from all my sin." That same faith needs to be expressed in your battle with any sinful addiction. "Lord, I cannot do this in my own strength. I am so worthless and weak. Please, Lord, give me the strength these next few hours to say no to every temptation I face. I want to take each step (to walk) in a way that is pleasing to You. Do not let me wander, walk, or take another step in a selfish, fleshly direction. Lord, I trust You to keep me from the temptations that I would yield to. I trust You to protect me from the wrong circumstances and wrong opportunities and to once again walk in the flesh. Help me to walk in the Spirit."

4. Strangle your sin! Don't let it breathe. Don't let it live!

This is what God says.

Colossians 3:5–7

Mortify therefore your members which are upon the earth; fornication, uncleanness, inordinate affection, evil concupiscence, and covetousness, which is idolatry: for which things' sake the wrath of God cometh on the children of disobedience: in the which ye also walked some time, when ye lived in them.

Now think about it.

Execute, murder, strangle, and put to death everything that belongs to your earthly nature, the sinful, worldly things that lurk within you; kill all sexual sin, pornography, premarital sex (fornication), impurity, filthiness (uncleanness), sensual lust (inordinate affection), shameful desires, and gross perversions (evil concupiscence). Put to death the covetousness and greed in your heart, which is nothing more than a longing for sensual things that are not yours to have, see, touch, or enjoy. Destroy the sexual idolatry that is living in your heart. Because of your disobedience and involvement with these things, the terrible wrath of God is coming. Just because you used to live in these sins before you trusted Christ as your Savior doesn't mean you have to anymore. Kill them all!

How can this affect me?

Some sins you can dig up by the roots and watch die. Other sins you have to put a stranglehold on them until they suffocate. Some sins you can starve to death by refusing to feed them on a daily basis. Other sins die from boredom as you completely ignore them. You know what sin you deal with and what it will take to kill it. It is not a matter of how to kill it, but are you *willing* to kill it? Please, dig down to the roots of your sinful addictions, cut them off, starve them, strangle them … kill them.

5. When temptation comes … run!
Run so fast and so far that the temptation cannot find you!
This is what God says.

Genesis 39:7–12

And it came to pass after these things, that his master's wife cast her eyes upon Joseph; and she said, Lie with me. But he refused, and said unto his master's wife, Behold, my master wotteth not what is with me in the house, and he hath committed all that he hath to my hand; there is none greater in this house than I; neither hath he kept back any thing from me but thee, because thou art his wife: how then can I do this great wickedness, and sin against God? And it came to pass, as she spake to Joseph day by day, that he hearkened not unto her, to lie by her, or to be with her. And it came to pass about this time, that Joseph went into the house to do his business; and there was none of the men of the house there within. And she caught him by his garment, saying, Lie with me: and he left his garment in her hand, and fled, and got him out.

Now think about it.

And after a while, Potiphar's wife took notice of Joseph and asked him to go to bed with her. But Joseph refused, saying, "Listen, my master Potiphar does not worry about anything in his entire house because he has given me authority over everything he has; because he trusts me so much, there is nobody in this house with more authority than I have. Potiphar has withheld nothing from my use and enjoyment except you because you are his wife! How do you expect me to betray your husband in such a wicked way and sin against God?" But that did not stop Potiphar's wife as she tried to seduce Joseph to go to bed with her day after day. He refused to sleep with her. In fact, he refused to even be around her. (He stayed as far away from the temptation as he could.) One day Joseph went into the house to do his work; and conveniently for Potiphar's wife, there was no one around. She was so insistent on going to bed with Joseph that she grabbed hold of his cloak, saying, "Come to bed with me." Joseph ran and got out of that house as fast as he could, but as he did, he left his cloak in her hand.

How can this affect me?

What would you have done? Would you have said yes to Potiphar's wife the first time she asked you to sleep with her? How would you have faced work every day knowing that she was going to try to seduce you once again? Would you have done everything you could have to stay away from her? Joseph could have made excuses for sleeping with her like "Well, she is my authority so I had better do what she wants." "If I don't listen to her, she will have me killed!" "Hey, why not, no one will ever know." But Joseph refused to sleep with her. He stayed away from her as much as he could. When she grabbed hold of him and the temptation was at its peak, he simply ran. Joseph was not consumed with pleasing his own fleshly desires. He kept his focus on pleasing God. In a way, Potiphar's wife is still hanging around today. She is calling to you from television, movies, websites, school, or work. If you face these temptations "day by day," simply follow Joseph's example. Keep your focus on your Lord and RUN!

6. Remember, God is more than enough! Be content with His presence and discontent with your sin!

This is what God says.

Hebrews 13:4–5

Marriage is honourable in all, and the bed undefiled: but whoremongers and adulterers God will judge. Let your conversation be without covetousness; and be content with such things as ye have: for he hath said, I will never leave thee, nor forsake thee.

Now think about it.

Marriage between a man and a woman should be honored, respected, and esteemed by all, and the marriage bed kept pure, holy, special, and undefiled from infidelity and unfaithfulness. But mark it down, adulterers and those who crave sex outside of marriage, those consumed with sex in thought and entertainment, those who live almost every waking moment seeking ways to satisfy their fleshly desires, those who live immoral lives addicted to sex (whoremongers) God will surely judge. (You cannot mess around with illicit sex on any level and escape the judgment of God. If you are His child, chastisement will come. You will not get away with your sin. God promises that He will not overlook it and let you get by.) Live your life without covetousness (constantly desiring that which God never intended you to have, always desiring more and more, thinking that you never have enough); and be content with what you have; be satisfied with what God has already given you (this also includes your spouse or your future spouse) for God has said, "Never will I leave you; never will I forsake you."

How can this affect me?

Sex is not dirty or sinful in the confines of marriage. Marriage between a man and a woman is God's righteous (right) way of satisfying sexual desires. Sex in marriage is an unselfish way to satisfy your partner, not a selfish way to satisfy yourself. Contentment is the key. Covetousness is the curse. If you constantly desire what you do not have, you will live in the sorrow of discontent. If you are thankful for what God has given you, you can live in the joy of contentment. God has given you everything you need for your present happiness. God is more than enough. Be content with God and His promised presence, and you will be able to step back from the edge of sexual addiction. You can!

7. If you fall . . . repeat steps 1 through 7!

Proverbs 24:16

For a just man falleth seven times, and riseth up again: but the wicked shall fall into mischief.

Now It's Your Turn

Now, it's your turn to meditate.

Using the same format we have followed for the last 18 meditations, write your own meditation and application for the passages listed in our final chapter. Refer back to the chapter on the mechanics of meditation and please do not get in a hurry. Using word studies and a good study Bible, meditate on each passage listed to fully understand what God is saying to you and then apply it in such a way that your heart stays pure. Enjoy your meditation.

This is what God says.

Proverbs 15:26

The thoughts of the wicked are an abomination to the Lord: but the words of the pure are pleasant words.

Now think about it.

_____

_____

_____

_____

_____

_____

_____

_____

_____

How can this affect me?

_____

_____

_____

_____

_____

_____

_____

_____

_____

_____

This is what God says.

Titus 2:11–14

For the grace of God that bringeth salvation
hath appeared to all men, teaching us that, de-
nying ungodliness and worldly lusts, we should
live soberly, righteously, and godly, in this present world; looking for that blessed hope, and
the glorious appearing of the great God and our
Savior Jesus Christ; who gave himself for us, that
he might redeem us from all iniquity, and purify
unto himself a peculiar people, zealous of good
works.

Now think about it.

_____

_____

_____

_____

_____

_____

_____

_____

_____

How can this affect me?

_____

_____

_____

_____

_____

_____

_____

_____

_____

_____

This is what God says.

Isaiah 26:3

Thou wilt keep him in perfect peace, whose mind is stayed on thee: because he trusteth in thee.

Now think about it.

_____

_____

_____

_____

_____

_____

_____

_____

_____

How can this affect me?

_____

_____

_____

_____

_____

_____

_____

_____

_____

This is what God says.

Psalm 119:9–16

Wherewithal shall a young man cleanse his way? by taking heed thereto according to thy word. With my whole heart have I sought thee: O let me not wander from thy commandments. Thy word have I hid in mine heart, that I might not sin against thee. Blessed art thou, O Lord: teach me thy statutes. With my lips have I declared all the judgments of thy mouth. I have rejoiced in the

way of thy testimonies, as much as in all riches.
I will meditate in thy precepts, and have respect
unto thy ways. I will delight myself in thy statutes: I will not forget thy word.

Now think about it.

_____

_____

_____

_____

_____

_____

_____

_____

How can this affect me?

_____

_____

_____

_____

_____

_____

_____

_____

_____

This is what God says.

Psalm 119:36–37

Incline my heart unto thy testimonies, and not to covetousness. Turn away mine eyes from beholding vanity; and quicken thou me in thy way.

Now think about it.

_____

_____

_____

_____

_____

_____

_____

How can this affect me?

_____

_____

_____

_____

_____

_____

_____

_____

Take heed,

watch out,

be careful . . .

Lest you fall